*Cover image by*
*http://www.aerox.net/*

Internet
Income

*Courtesy Allposters.com*

## About This Text

This text was designed to provide everything you need to know about creating a steady income from the internet. Over the years I have developed a system that utilizes web sites combined with pay per click ads, affiliate ads, e-books and more, to create a steady inflow of paychecks from the web. Whether you have an existing brick and mortar business and just want to supplement your cash flow, want to work from home or plan on publishing a new website, I will show you how to create internet income. This text includes a wide variety of topics and ideas for web based profit centers. The majority of this text is devoted to those who want to develop an income producing web site or make an existing website more profitable. Please be advised this text does not contain any get rich quick schemes. You will have to do some work up front, but the end result can be monthly checks and deposits from a variety of sources to enhance or possibly replace your current income. Within this text I have listed many of the ways you can make money on the internet. You could spend years experimenting with each and finding out if they work or not. I will show you which sources I have used and which have been successful and consistently profitable. You can check out working examples of each and decide for yourself which ones you want to pursue. Most people who have a steady 9-5 job never realize the true income producing potential of the internet. You do not have to be a web site designer or graphic artist to succeed. All you have to have is a little ambition and set aside a few hours each week to develop your website and associated profit centers.

I highly advise reading the entire text cover to cover. Although users could certainly benefit from individual sections, reading the entire text will better prepare you to succeed and maximize online profits. I have listed below a few samples of how specific topics within this text can be utilized for your own specific needs.

**For existing business and web site owners;**
*Learn how to make money by placing ads on your web site, promoting new internet based products and using the power of the internet to market your own online products. For example, most webmasters could easily benefit from adding a related downloadable product to their existing web site and earning up to 70% profit without incurring any inventory cost and with no shipping and handling hassles. Sound to good to be true? Its not, just check out the sections listed below for details.*

> **Affiliate products:** How they can enhance your existing product line.
> **eBook promotion:** You can make 70% profit with no investment.
> **Pay per click (PPC) ads:** Ad revenue can increase monthly cash flow.
> **Pay per click Marketing:** Increase traffic to your website.
> **e-mail marketing:** A great way to promote products and services.
> **Online Auctions:** Learn how to sell products and promote your business.
> **Blogs & forums:** Learn to drive customers to your site.

**For people who want to create a profitable new web site;**
*Anyone with a little imagination and creativity can learn how to develop a profitable web site. This text will teach you all the tricks of the trade that make the*

*job easy. All text is written in plain english and designed for regular people (not computer programmers) to understand. Check out what topics you will learn about in this book.*

**Domain name:** Picking the right name can be very important.
**Hosting package:** Choosing the best package.
**Unique content:** The importance of unique content.
**Web design:** How to create a site designed to make money.
**Affiliate products:** Learn to promote and profit from these products.
**eBook Promotion:** You can make 70% profit with no investment.
**eBook Publishing:** Produce an eBook and learn to market it through other affiliates.
**Print on Demand Publishing:** How to turn your eBook into a soft cover book with Print on demand publishing
**Pay per click (PPC) ad revenue:** Ad revenue can increase your monthly cash flow.
**Pay per click advertising:** Increase traffic to your web site.
**Tracking:** Learn how to keep track of your traffic.
**e-mail marketing:** A great way to promote products and services.
**Online auctions:** Learn to sell product and promote your website at the same time.

**For individuals who want to work from home**
*Do you just need a little extra cash? Do you already have a job but just want to enhance your current salary? Don't want to set up your own website but would love to be able to earn money from the comfort of your own home. Check out these online money making opportunities.*

**Online surveys:** How to make money by filling out surveys.
**Surfing the web:** How to profit from surfing the web and reading email.

*Surf the web and make money from the comfort of your own home. Image courtesy AllPosters.com. See affiliate section for additional information on how you can profit from these photographs and art images.*

*www.WebMoneyExpo.com*

## About The Author

Daniel Berg worked in the SCUBA industry for over twenty years. He owned and operated Aqua Explorers Inc. a wholesale distribution company. Mr. Berg has authored over a dozen shipwreck and diving related books and was the host and producer of the award winning Dive Wreck Valley TV series. Capt. Dan received the prestigious BTS Diver of the Year Award in 1994. He was also a first year recipient of the SSI Platinum Pro 5000 Award. Mr. Berg holds 6 US patents for diving equipment design. His photographs, video and articles have appeared on Fox 5 News, CNN, CBS, Skin Diver Magazine, plus many more. The author did not develop his system for creating internet income overnight. Over the past ten years he has constantly expanded and refined a variety of internet profit centers. Mr. Berg has now complied all of his tricks of the trade into this realistic how to guide. Unlike other web profit programs Mr. Berg makes no grandiose claims. He shows readers how he has and continues to create internet income and how you can do the same. Please note that his web sites which are often used as examples are usually based on his scuba, boating or other areas of interest.

## *Topics*

### Creating a Profitable Web Site

Domain Name
Web Hosting
Website Design
Page Layout/Unique Content
Headings
Page Templet
Tables
Background
Things to Avoid
Optimization
Unique Content
Links
Meta Tags
Page Title
Keywords
Description
Photos
Website Submission
Tracking Website Traffic
Web Page Analyzer
Web Page Optimization

### Web Site Promotion

Search Engine Submission
Blogs
Forums
Pay per click Advertising
YouTube
News Release
Pay per sale Marketing
Opt in Mailing List
Affiliate Marketing

### Profiting from Your web Site

Pay per click ad Revenue
Affiliate Programs
ebook Marketing

---

---

Learn how to produce, market or sell already published eBooks.
ebook Publishing
Publish your own eBook and profit from having your own affiliate network promote your product.
Kindle Electronic Readers
How to profit from this exciting technology
Print on Demand Products
Book Publishing
Learn how to profit from turning your eBooks into a published soft cover book.

Online  Auctions
Advertisements
Once you have significant traffic you can sell ads on your website.

## Web Commerce Tools and Services

e-Commerce
List of online sites you can utilize for your internet business.
Victual Cash
Services that allow your customers to pay for product and services online.
Free Clipart
Free clipart and images you can use to enhance your products or web site.

## Make Money by Surfing the Web

Online  Surveys
Earn money by taking online surveys.
Surf the web
Make money by reading emails and surfing the web.

*Image courtesy AllPosters.com. See Affiliate section for additional information on how you can profit from these photographs and art images.*

## CREATING A PROFITABLE WEB SITE

Follow my simple instructions and design a website that can create profits for years to come. The first step is deciding on a topic and then creating unique content text for that site. Unique content is just one of the main factors to creating successful and long lasting internet profits. With a website you will be able to market your own products, place pay per click advertising and market affiliate products. The key to success with any web page is traffic or page views. Its all basically about percentages. If you can generate enough visitor traffic to your website a certain percentage of these people will click on the ads or buy the products that you will be promoting. It use to be that webmasters could quickly put up a site and just post links to other true content sites. Now it's nearly impossible for link directory type sites to succeed. It's highly

advised to pick a website topic that you are interested in, or already an expert in and then spend the time to research and write quality, useful unique content about that topic. Think about writing the text as if you were writing a college paper, article or writing your own book. Your web site should be informative and accurate. Give the end user a reason to want to come back time and time again. Web sites can be made for almost any topic. If you are a stock broker you could write about investing, and related topics like retirement planning. If you are currently working as a carpenter you could create a how to site about home improvements and include all of your tricks of the trade. Each related topic could be it's own page within your website. Once you have created a basic website you can always continue to add to it and enhance its content. Once your web site is finished you will then have to work on generating traffic to it. This can be done through search engines, through links from other similar topic websites, blogs, forums, through affiliates, and by advertising. Sound like its getting a little complicated. Don't worry I will cover each topic in detail.

Before we get started I want to emphasize the importance of unique

*Courtesy Allposters.com*

content. The bottom line is that your web site will have a much better chance of obtaining top search engine performance and therefore more traffic and better profitability, if your content is unique and popular. For example, you may not do well, even if you have a beautifully designed website, if the topic is so obscure that not many people search for related key words. On the other hand you could write about a very popular subject, but not get top search engine placement, because of the amount of competition or similar web sites on the same subject. The key to success is to create a site that is truly worthwhile to readers. I write content as if I were writing a book.

### Basic steps to creating a profitable web page
*1) Buy a keyword rich domain name.*
*2) Write unique content text.*
*3) Purchase a hosting package.*
*4) Design and produce pages.*
*5) Add photos.*
*6) Use Meta Tags (title, description and keywords).*
*7) Add pay per click ads like.*

*www.WebMoneyExpo.com*

*Google adsense*
*8) Join Paypal*
*9) Add Affiliate products*
 *CJ.com*
 *Clickbank*
 *amazon.com*
 *Allposters*
*10) ebook publishing*
*11) Print on demand products*
 *Lulu*
 *Cafepress*
*12) Page optimization*
*13) Site Submission*
*14) Add Tracking*
*15) Page Analyzer*
*16) Promote your site*
 *Search engine submission*
 *Pay per click advertising*
 *Opt in email marketing*
 *Youtube*
 *ebay*
 *blogs*
 *forums*
 *news release*
 *links*

### Domain Name

The first step in creating a website is to buy a domain name. Many companies offer free domain names if you host the site with them. Others will require you to purchase the domain name. In either case search for an available name that will quickly identify your web sites content topic. You should also pick a name that is keyword rich. Think about how people will search and find your website and pick a name that utilizes some of these keyword search terms. For example, my sites domain name, www.WebMoneyExpo.com, and associated description can be found by those using search engines much easier than if I had picked a random name like WMEinc.com

### Web Hosting

After you have secured a domain name, it's time to purchase a hosting package. Below you will find a list of several internet hosting companies. All are very highly rated. I have found that it is often alot easier to use the same service for web hosting as you did to purchase your domain name. (*Please note that this is not a complete list of hosting services but rather some of the more popular services at the time of this writing*).

Godaddy                    http://www.godaddy.com/
*Enhance your site with today's hottest hosting applications and utilities. Godaddy is the company that I used for domain and hosting. They are very easy to work with and have an excellent customer support system.*

Inmotion                    http://www.inmotion.com/
*Inmotion web hosting network is based on the fast and reliable Linux and Unix operating systems. It is monitored 24/7.*

Justhost                    http://www.justhost.com/
*Justhost web hosting prides themselves on  commitment to customers and want to make sure they have all the details they need before making that big decision.*

Webhostingpad                    http://www.webhostingpad.com/
*Web Hosting Pad provides a fast, reliable and comprehensive service.*

Fatcow                    http://www.fatcow.com/
*The Original FatCow Web hosting will provide you with good service and help you every step of the way.*

Supergreen                    http://www.supergreen.com/
*There are many reasons why so many people choose Super Green over any other web hosting. Whether you're a beginner or an experienced webmaster, Supergreen offers the perfect solution for everyone*

Greengeeks                    http://www.greengeeks.com/
*Your site will be placed on high quality, name brand Intel Dual Quad Core servers with RAID-10 storage technology for  fast and reliable hosting service.*

*Courtesy Allposters.com*

Bluehost                http://www.bluehost.com/
*From the business owner to the individual who desires full functionality on a small budget, Bluehost provides your complete web hosting solution*

Hostmonster         http://www.hostmonster.com/
*Hostmonster has been providing hosting solutions to thousands of business and personal web sites since 1996. Their internet hosting package helps businesses and individuals get high-powered service at a fraction of the cost*

Yahoo                http://www.yahoo.com
*Yahoo! is committed to making your online business a success. To prove they offer the best web hosting plan, they offer a 30-Day Satisfaction Guarantee! If you're not completely happy with your service within 30 days of ordering Yahoo Web Hosting, They will refund your hosting fee*

## Web Page Design

There are two different schools of thought when it comes to website design. Some recommend hiring a professional design firm or graphic artist. You would then end up with a truly professional looking web page. In many cases your web page will be the first impression with potential customers so making a good and professional first impression is extremely important. The down side is that anytime you want to change the design or content

you will have to go through a middleman or webmaster and their may be charges. Many software programs now make it relatively easy to create your own web page. Creating your own pages allows you total creative control and the ability to update the site, its content and related ads, affiliate products and other profit centers without incurring any cost. Many web hosting services also offer free web design programs. These programs have standard templates that allow even the beginner to quickly and easily publish a professional looking web site. I use Microsoft Front Page software to create all of my web pages. Front Page requires a slight learning curve but with a little experience anyone can quickly produce professional looking web pages. The added benefit of being your own webmaster is that you will be able to use the same design program to export HTML code and greatly enhance the design of your online auctions and email marketing newsletters. Either way you choose, I highly recommend learning some basic HTML code. You will need to know the basics to insert images, create hyperlinks, and do some other basic text formatting.

*Creating a profitable web site. Image courtesy AllPosters.com. See affiliate section for additional information on how you can profit from these photographs and art images.*

*Samples of web page design software*
Microsoft FrontPage®
Adobe GoLive®
Adobe Dreamweaver®
Microsoft Publisher
Most FTP software

**Page Layout /Content**
The design and page layout of any web page is very important. Page layout can cause a page to look professional or can have completely the opposite effect. Page design can even have an impact on search engine results. Search engines read a pages text from top to bottom. Therefore, make sure you utilize your main keywords and keyword phrases near the beginning of your content text. You should make sure that important text is positioned before non key word related text like your street address, phone number or links to other websites. Some search engines ignore meta tags and gather information about your site directly from your web page text.

*Courtesy Allposters.com*

They will use the first 100-200 characters of text as the description displayed with its search results. As with meta tags it's important to position your main keywords and keyword phrases at the beginning of your content text. For additional information on the importance of keywords refer to the Meta Tag section of this text. Main keywords can and should be used as headers for paragraphs. Some search engines will place special emphasis on text used as a header that is bold and in a larger font than the balance of the content.

The number of times a keyword is mentioned in the content text of a page can also have a positive effect on ranking. Please do not try to outsmart the search engines. Do not for example repeat a word over and over. Some search engines consider this spamming and it will greatly reduce your chance of obtaining higher page rank. I suggest using original content text rich in keywords that are appropriate and make sense. If it does not sound good when you proof read your text, do not use it.

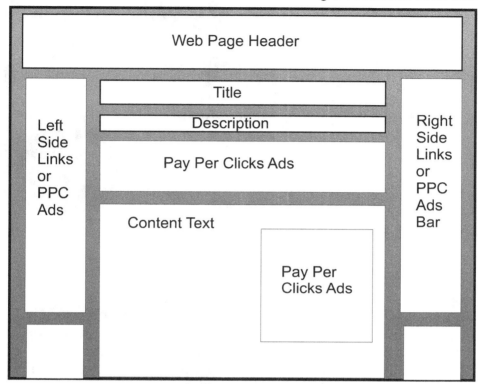

**Page Template**

Most web design software programs give the user the ability to use templates. Templates are basically a standard design format that you set up one time and then can use on as may pages as you desire. The benefit comes not only from making each page uniform in design but making multiple pages easy to produce. You can incorporate navigation links, pay per click advertising and tracking services directly into your page templet. This way all you have to do for each page is create a title, description, and unique content text. I highly advise spending a little time up-front and learning to use templates before designing your first web page.

*Sample template the author set up on Microsoft FrontPage. Note fields for title, description, photos and product text*

Title

Description

Page Text

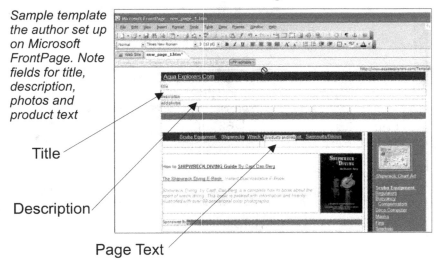

**Tables**

As you start to design your first web page you will find that it is often easier to work with tables. Tables can be used in a variety of ways. They can have background colors, borders or just control the placement of text within a desired area. I often create a template with tables. The tables are used for design as well as organization. Take a look at the illustration above. Each area of the template was designed with tables. For example the title, description and page text fields on this template were each created with a simple table.

*Courtesy Allposters.com*

## Headings
Many search engines put special emphasis on text that is used as a header. Headings should be in larger print and should be bold. If possible use your main keyword or keyword phrases as headers.

## Background
The background of a web page can be plain white, colored or can use a graphic. For example, some sites incorporate their company logo or an associated design into background art. The use of this type of graphic background is entirely based on the artistic value and has no effect on search engine results.

## Things to avoid
Here is a simple list of things not to do when designing your web page. It's very simple, search engines do not like and may penalize you if your web page contains any of the following:

*Never use hidden text: Do not use text that is either too small or is the same color as the background.*

*Never use an excessive amount of keywords.*

*Do not copy content. Never copy content from another web site.*

*No word spamming: Don't repeat a word over and over over.*

*Do not make pages comprised of just a graphic image with no content text.*

*Do not use large image files. A slow loading page may appear to be broken and may be excluded by some search engines.*

*Sites must be available at the time the search engine spiders it or it will be excluded.*

*Do not use "Under Construction". Some search engines do not want to list sites that are not complete.*

*Never use symbols in the URL: Sites that have symbols like ampersand (&), percent sign (%), equals sign (=), dollar sign ($) or question mark (?).*

*Do not post pages that have no content but only link to other pages or domains.*

*Do not post illegal content*

*Be careful about where you have your pages hosted. If the hosting service also hosts spammers and pornographers, you could wind up being penalized or excluded simply because the underlying IP address for that service is the same for all the virtual domains it includes.*

*Courtesy Allposters.com*

---

*Creating a profitable web site. Image courtesy AllPosters.com. See Affiliate section for additional information on how you can profit from these photographs and art images.*

## Web Page Optimization

Search Engine Optimization (SEO) is a process to maximize your website performance. There are pages of information on the web that deal with website page optimization. Some are very technical and others provide information that is outdated. Below you will find the basics that will hopefully lead you to develop a content based web page that obtains high ranking on the major search engines. Some key factors that must be considered when dealing with page optimization are the site's Meta Tags (title, keywords, description), content and actual use of keywords in the content of the page. Remember, it's all about percentages. The more page views your site gets the more people will click on your ads and buy the products you are promoting. One of the best ways to get traffic is from the major search engines. You want a potential customer to be able to type a keyword into a search engines search box and come up with your website. At the time of this writing the main search engine is Google. In fact, many believe that Google has a monopoly

*Courtesy Allposters.com*

on the service. In any case getting a high page ranking on Google can certainly result in dramatically increased traffic to your website. Although, this may sound pretty easy it can actually be quite difficult. The problem that many have faced is that Google changes its algorithm fairly often and noone ever knows exactly what they are looking for. For example, in the past many web sites were ranked high based on their link popularity. Search engines counted the number of links into and out of each site to determine this popularity. Webmasters, quickly learned that they could swap links with other webmasters, regardless of the sites content and obtain better search engine page rank. As a result search engines found they had high ranked sites listed which had no content. They were just directory sites loaded with links. Anyway, to make a long story short some search engines changed their algorithms so search results showed sites with true value. The bottom line is that it can be quite tricky to get top ranked. If you read the forums, many webmasters go crazy constantly changing their web site design,

*Courtesy Allposters.com*

links, even content in a never ending battle to stay top ranked. Instead, I recommend a very simple approach. Use the basic guidelines listed below for designing a quality content rich website. Then leave it alone and concentrate on marketing your online products and or services.

### Unique Content

Design your site for your customers not the search engines. Perhaps the most important feature of any web site is original content and useful information that makes users want to return again and again. You should write the text or content for your web site like you were writing a well researched book. You will learn additional income producing benefits of quality content in later sections when we cover ebooks and print on demand products. For now each topic can become its own page within your website.

### Links

The key to success for a website is good search engine ranking. All of the major search engines use some degree of link popularity to determine how well a site will rank - so the more high quality, relevant one way links that lead to your site, the higher it should rank. Unfortunately, reciprocal links could be a thing of the past. Apparently, Google now only credits one way links into your site toward page rank. I now try to avoid exchanging links and only link to other quality web sites with very similar topics. If your content is unique and of true value to the end user then other webmasters will link to your site without requiring a reciprocal link in return.

When designing your web page keep in mind that you should only have a maximum of 100 links per page. This includes internal and external links.

### Meta Tags

Meta Tags are part of a websites HTML code. They are a very important part of web page optimization. Meta tags are used by most search engines to gather their information about your company and the services you provide. This information is used by many search engines to determine when your site should be included in search results and where your site will be placed in those results. They may not be the magic answer but they can have a lot of influence. There are many types of Meta tags but the most important are keywords, page description and title. Most web page design software list all under page properties.

### *Page Title*

Your website's title can have a major influence on where your website appears in any specific search engine's results. It is very important to use your most important keyword or keyword phrase as the first words in your title. Many sites choose to use a company name as the title but in most cases this will not benefit your site regarding search engine results.

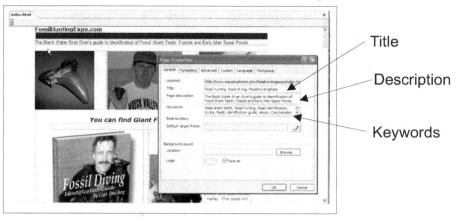

Title

Description

Keywords

*Meta Tags, listed under page properties. Sample is of the authors Fossil Hunting web site which promotes an ebook and print on demand book.*

Limit your title meta tag to no more than 100 letters. Put your most important keyword phrase first. Remember a good website meta tag title should be brief, keyword rich and targeted to your sites content.

### Key words

Keywords are words or phrases that people could use when searching for your site. Keyword metatags are also one of the areas that most search engines will use to gather information about your web site. The major search engines will take your keyword metatags and store them in their memory, so they know when your site should be brought up in search results. You should make a list of keywords for each and every page in your web site. Each page should have a different keywords list that relates to that page's specific content. Start listing single words or short phrases that you think you or others would use to search when trying to find your products or service. You should list 20 to 100 words or phrases. Always try to list your keywords as key phrases, meaning two or more words long. Usually, there are hundreds or even thousands of other sites that will have similar topics and keywords. If you use phrases of two or more words, you will have a better chance of being located during a web search. I highly suggest that you use the main keyword or phrase first in the meta tag key word list. List the remainder of your keywords and key phrases from the most important to the least important. Some search engines only use a limited number of keywords from your site, therefore, you do not want to have your most important words or phrases excluded because they were towards the end of your meta tag list. It's better to focus on fewer key word  phrases rather than using hundreds of keywords. Some search engines use a scoring method. They basically place less value on a keyword which is part of 200 total keywords compared to the same keyword which is part of only 30 total keywords. Never use ALL CAPS in your keyword meta tags. Some search engines are case sensitive, which means a search  for "Scuba" would return different results than a search for "scuba."  Remember key words should also be used prominently in the pages title, the domain name, and throughout the sites unique content text.

### Description

A website Description is the text that shows up next to your title in search engines results. Description should be one or two sentences and should tell what your website is about and what services you provide.  Not all search engines show the same amount of description text in their search results. Some use 60 characters  while others will use upwards of  200 characters. Therefore it is very important to be concise and to the point. Whenever possible use your primary keywords or phrases in your page description.

## Photos
Photographs, video and graphic files can be very large and can slow down the function of a web site. Try to keep photo and image file size under control. It should not take more than a few seconds

to open any page. If you have AOL for your email I use a very simple technique to resize images. Just copy and paste any image or group of images into the text of an email. Then send the email to yourself. AOL will automatically ask if you want to optimize the image. Click on yes. Then open the received email and save the photo.

Name all photos with relevant key words that describe the image. This way web surfers can find your website when they are searching for images as well as for content.

## Tracking Website Traffic
Anyone with a web site should be able to track where visitors, or potential customers came from. With this information you can work on problem areas or capitalize on strategies that are working. In either case knowledge is the key. For example, by adding a simple tracking code to each of your web pages you would know how many hits were obtained from an email marketing campaign or which search engine is providing the most traffic. You will even be able to tell which key words are being used in order for your customers to find your web page. To start I recommend one of the free tracking services. I use eXTREeMe Tracker. With the eXTReMe Tracker you get every advanced feature required to picture the visitors of your website. Conveniently arranged, numbers, percentages, stats, totals and averages.

| Referrer Totals: Searchengines | | |
|---|---|---|
| Google | 128225 | 61.94% |
| Yahoo | 35209 | 17.01% |
| MSN Search | 23611 | 11.41% |
| Google Images | 6149 | 2.97% |
| AOL Search | 5426 | 2.62% |
| Live.com | 3255 | 1.57% |
| Bing.com | 2586 | 1.25% |
| Dogpile | 1037 | 0.50% |

*Sample information available once eXTReMe tracker is set up on your web site.*

www.WebMoneyExpo.com

| Hours of the Day | | | |
|---|---|---|---|
| 00:00 - 00:59 | 15527 | 5.71% | |
| 01:00 - 01:59 | 16668 | 6.13% | |
| 02:00 - 02:59 | 17654 | 6.49% | |
| 03:00 - 03:59 | 16320 | 6.00% | |
| 04:00 - 04:59 | 12131 | 4.46% | |
| 05:00 - 05:59 | 7609 | 2.80% | |
| 06:00 - 06:59 | 4604 | 1.69% | |
| 07:00 - 07:59 | 2927 | 1.08% | |
| 08:00 - 08:59 | 1970 | 0.72% | |
| 09:00 - 09:59 | 1710 | 0.63% | |
| 10:00 - 10:59 | 1790 | 0.66% | |
| 11:00 - 11:59 | 2437 | 0.90% | |
| 12:00 - 12:59 | 4383 | 1.61% | |
| 13:00 - 13:59 | 7386 | 2.72% | |
| 14:00 - 14:59 | 11000 | 4.05% | |
| 15:00 - 15:59 | 13423 | 4.94% | |
| 16:00 - 16:59 | 15409 | 5.67% | |
| 17:00 - 17:59 | 16506 | 6.07% | |
| 18:00 - 18:59 | 16858 | 6.20% | |
| 19:00 - 19:59 | 17943 | 6.60% | |
| 20:00 - 20:59 | 18328 | 6.74% | |
| 21:00 - 21:59 | 18118 | 6.66% | |
| 22:00 - 22:59 | 16316 | 6.00% | |
| 23:00 - 23:59 | 14836 | 5.46% | |

*Tracking software provides web masters with a wealth of information. Once you can see when and where your traffic is coming from you can plan strategies to improve of enhance that traffic .*

To insert Tracker onto your own website just click on the link listed below.
http://extremetracking.com
Sign up for a free account and then copy and paste the HTML code onto your website. I usually set up a template for each website. I then paste the Tracker code to the bottom of my template page. This way the Tracker will automatically appear on every page which utilizes the template. After the Tracker code is in place you can easily click on the Tracker logo on any page to check your stats.

Please note that eXTREeMe Tracker is not the only tracking software available. This is the system I have used and have always found the information provided to be reliable and very useful.

### Web Page Analyzer/ Link Checker
There are quite a few web page analyzation services available on the web. Once you have published your website I recommend using a site like those listed below. Just cut and past your web page URL into the free analyzer and it will provide an online report with details

on how you can improve your site.

http://analyze.websiteoptimization.com/wso
http://www.sitesolutions.com

You should also periodically check your site for broken links. Many search engines count bad or broken links against you when organizing your position in search results. Again many services are available. I use dead links because it's fast, easy and most importantly free.

http://www.dead-links.com/

*Promoting your
web site.
Courtesy
Allposters.com*

## Promoting your Web Site

There are many ways to promote or market your website. The first and often most successful is through search engines. We have already discussed unique content, meta tags and site optimization. Now let's look at some other ways to increase traffic by promoting your web page.

### Web Site Submission

Once your website is published you should submit your sites URL to Yahoo, Google, ASK, MSN and other search engines. This is easier than it sounds. I use a free service http://websitesubmit.hypermart.net/freesubmit.htm

All you have to do is copy and paste your web site URL into web submits text box and hit submit. As a rule, I always open my web page and then highlight and copy the URL. This way I can paste the URL and avoid any possible typographical errors. After submitting your page, you will receive a few e-mails that ask for confirmation. Respond to each and your sight will be found on the search engines pretty quickly. At first you may not rank high so do not expect much traffic That will come with time.

Google search results for "new jersey beach diver". Note the authors web site comes up first for a search of this key word phrase.

## Blogging

According to Wikipedia "a blog is usually maintained with regular entries of commentary, descriptions of events, or other material such as graphics or video". Entries are commonly displayed in reverse-chronological order. Blogs are a great way to generate interest in your web site and keep people coming back time and time again. Remember, traffic is the key to success. By building traffic that is interested in the content of your web site through a blog you will definitely see profit from your pay per click advertising and product sales. There are different types of Blogging software available. I like  http://wordpress.org/ which is free and makes setting up a blog on your web site easy to install and use.
I also recommend setting up blog categories. Most blog software allows you to create sub-categories to help organize your entries. This will help visitors narrow in on specific interests.

*Pay Per Click Marketing.*
*Your ad appears here.*
*You pay everyt ime someone clicks on your ad.*

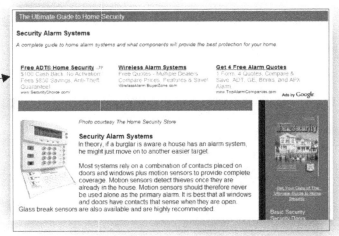

### Forums

According to Wikipedia, an Internet forum, or message board, is an online discussion site. Forums originated as the modern equivalent of a traditional bulletin board. For the purpose of promoting your website, forums are an excellent tool to help drive traffic to your domain. You can benefit from existing forums or create your own. In either case you will have to consistently create topics or comment on others. I basically set up a spread sheet and list topic related forums. I then sign up to each and either post a topic or respond to another post. In either case I usually reference information on one of my web pages. If the forum generates a lot of response than I move it to the top of my spread sheet (under that topic). This way I know which forums to concentrate my efforts in the future. If you decide to create your own forum you can also benefit from posting affiliate ads, and pay per click ads on the same site. In either case the goal is to drive traffic to your web site and associated ads and products.

### Pay Per Click Marketing

Pay per click marketing can be an excellent way to obtain traffic for your website. Google Adwords is the best known program but many programs are now available. Basically, you pay for each click to an ad that you create. These ads are shown on others websites and

Pay per click advertising can be an excellent way to obtain traffic for your web site. Google Adwords is the best known program but many programs are now available. Basically, you pay for each click to an ad created to market your product or service.

are designed to market your product or service. I highly recommend adding Tracking URLs to any site that uses pay per click marketing. With tracking and the information provided from Google you can determine your sales and what your net income is per click. For example, after a trial period say one month just calculate the profit per click. With this information you will know if you can afford to continue your PPC marketing campaign. You will also be able to do an equal and balanced comparison of different PPC marketing vendors to determine which works best for you. Remember, keep your eye on the bottom line and never pay more per click than you make.

### YouTube

Try to think outside the box when it comes to website marketing. One example is to post a short video on YouTube which details any new product or that highlights the content of your site. These short

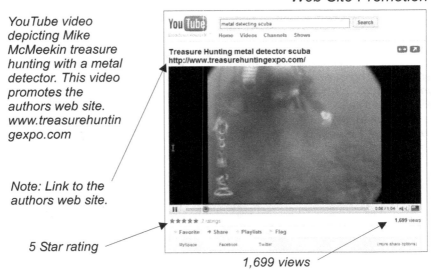

*YouTube video depicting Mike McMeekin treasure hunting with a metal detector. This video promotes the authors web site. www.treasurehuntin gexpo.com*

*Note: Link to the authors web site.*

*5 Star rating*

*1,699 views*

videos can get quite a bit of exposure and best of all they are free to post. Remember to provide a link to your website so interested viewers can visit your web page and therefore increase your traffic and profits

### News Release
Anytime you have a new product, host an event or update information you should make an announcement. One great way to do this is to make up a New Release mailing list (either email and or snail mail). For example, if you created a new ebook about skydiving you could write a news release and send it to outdoor and sky diving related magazines. In most cases these publications are looking for text and will print your news release word for word for free. Best part is the reader looks at this text as editorial rather than as a paid advertisement. Remember to provide the URL for your web site and any applicable ordering information.

### Pay Per Sale Marketing
If you have your own product you may want to consider marketing it through a pay per sale marketing program. You would basically offer your product though an affiliate vendor. Other web masters could

then join the same program and offer your product direct to their online customers. They would make a commission for each item sold. You would benefit from the increased exposure and sales. See Affiliate section of this text. Many of the same vendors that offer affiliate programs can also market your unique product.

Check out
www.cj.com

*Sample of one of the authors new product News Releases. Magazines are always looking for text and will often print your news release word for word, for free. The best aspect of a new release is that the reader looks at this text as editorial rather than as a paid advertisement. Remember to provide the URL for your web site and any applicable ordering information.*

# News.................... for immediate release please.

Attention Editor,

## New Treasure Hunting Book

Aqua Explorers Inc. would like to announce the release of Capt. Dan Berg's latest book, **Beach and Water Treasure Hunting with Metal Detectors.** A complete how to guide to discovering lost jewelry and coins from the sand and water.

Capt. Dan has authored over a dozen shipwreck and diving related books. He hosted the Dive Wreck Valley cable TV series and actively walks the beach, water and scuba dives in search of lost jewelry and artifacts. Let Dan teach you all the tricks of the trade so you to can find Gold and Silver Treasure on any beach. This exciting new text includes sections on dry beach detecting, shallow surf, wading, scuba detecting and shipwreck diving. Treasure Hunting is available as a 70 page PDF ebook or as a soft cover perfect bound text. The book is packed with information and hundreds of images Ever go to the beach and watch a guy strolling down the waters edge metal detector in hand. That guy is not just searching for pocket change. He is looking for and most likely finding treasure. Learn why metal detecting can be enjoyed as a hobby by those of all ages. Its one of the only activities that can quickly pay for itself while providing the hobbyist with outdoor fun, adventure and exercise. This text teaches the basics as well as tricks of the trade learned form years of detecting. These techniques make it easy and will greatly increase your treasure hunting productivity. Anyone can discover lost gold and this book will show you how.

Book is available as a downloadable ebook for $9.95- http://www.treasurehuntingexpo.com/ or as Soft Cover perfect bound text - direct from our print on demand publisher http://www.lulu.com/product/paperback/beach-and-water-treasure-hunting-with-metal-detectors/5584247

Check out all of Capt. Dan's shipwreck and diving related books http://www.aquaexplorers.com/e_books_downloadable.htm

Sample Pages,
Images and review
copy available
on request

www.treasurehuntingexpo.com

Sincerely,
Capt. Daniel Berg

Aqua Explorers Inc. 2745 Cheshire Dr, Baldwin N.Y. 11510

*Most businesses can benefit greatly from generating their own mailing list of potential customers. These mailing lists contain the contact information of previous customers or those who have shown an interest in the companies products. Courtesy Allposters.com*

## Email Marketing

The internet is a unique marketplace that has endless possibilities but also a few basic rules to follow. Most business can benefit greatly from generating their own mailing list of potential customers. These mailing lists contain the contact information of previous customers or those who have shown an interest in the companies products. Internet entrepreneurs can also benefit but must be careful not to have their mailings classified as spam. One way to avoid this is to create an opt in/opt out mailing list. All this means is that individuals must sign on to the mailing list and have the option to have their name removed at any time. This type of mailing meats all of the internet's anti spam requirements. The added benefit is your mailings will be going to potential customers that have already shown an interest in your product. Many different companies offer Opt In mailing list services. some are more

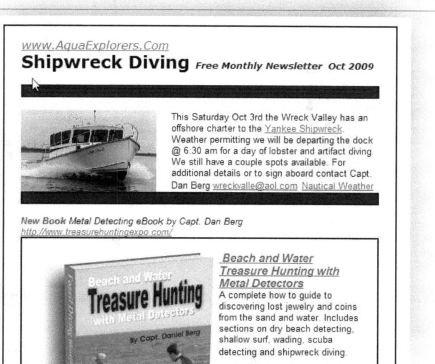

www.AquaExplorers.Com

# Shipwreck Diving  Free Monthly Newsletter  Oct 2009

This Saturday Oct 3rd the Wreck Valley has an offshore charter to the Yankee Shipwreck. Weather permitting we will be departing the dock @ 6:30 am for a day of lobster and artifact diving. We still have a couple spots available. For additional details or to sign aboard contact Capt. Dan Berg wreckvalle@aol.com Nautical Weather

New Book Metal Detecting eBook by Capt. Dan Berg
http://www.treasurehuntingexpo.com/

## Beach and Water Treasure Hunting with Metal Detectors
A complete how to guide to discovering lost jewelry and coins from the sand and water. Includes sections on dry beach detecting, shallow surf, wading, scuba detecting and shipwreck diving.

*Sample Newsletter used by the author with an Opt in email list to market new products and promote services.*

expensive than others. I would advise starting with a basic plan until you develop a large list of names. I currently use GoDaddy ( which is the same company I use for domain and hosting) and have found their email marketing plan affordable and fairly easy to use. They even have templates that help in designing a professional looking newsletter. I have also heard only good things about Constant Contacts Opt in program.

I have found that is actually easier to write and design the news release or newsletter in a web site design program. It just saves a little time and gives you a little more creativity and design flexibility. Once the layout is finished all I do is copy the HTML code from the design program directly onto Godaddy's email form. This process

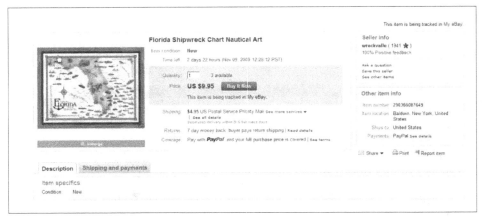

*Sample of one of the authors ebay auctions for a Shipwreck Chart Poster. For additional exposure to his web site the author posts links to his web page on all online auctions,*

saves quite a bit of time involved in individually uploading images.

## Think Outside the Box
You should promote your web site at every possible opportunity. The more visitors you get the better chance you have to make money. One idea is to post a link to your website on all of your outgoing emails. Another idea would be to post a link to your site on ebay, every time you auction a topic relevant product. Other ideas include putting a sign on your car. In any of these examples the added marketing value of thinking outside the box costs you nothing.

*Courtesy Allposters.com*

## Profiting from your Web Site

### Pay Per Click ad Revenue

One of the best ways to make money from your website is to post pay per click ads. Once in place you will get paid every time one of your customers clicks on an ad. No purchase is needed. Although, quite a few services now offer pay per click PPC programs, Google Adsense is still the premier program. Check out the Google advertisement at the top of www.webmoneyexpo.com. Google delivers ads like this that are appropriate for the content of your web site. It's referred to as contextual advertising. You get paid every time someone clicks on one of the ads. You can also customize the look of each of these ads so they match the design of your page. The first step is getting approved by Adsense. Before you even apply your website should be up and running for at least a few months. You should have at least 10-15 pages of unique content. Your content should not be copied from another site and you should not be promoting anything illegal or immoral.

*One of the authors web pages. I make money every time someone clicks on one of these pay per click ads. The same web page promotes one of the authors ebooks.*

Once approved for one site, you can place Adsense contextual ads on any site you own. You can decide to run just text ads or choose from a variety of image and text ad designs. Various sizes are also offered so it's usually pretty easy to fit an add into your web pages design.

*From*: Google Adsense
*Earn money while displaying advertisements on your website. When visitors click on these ads, Google pays you. Along with targeted advertising for your content pages, you can add a Google search box to your site and show targeted ads on search result pages.*

At the time of this writing Google Adsense is still the premier pay per click ad provider. Google can provide the most consistent content related ads, which means more clicks and therefore more revenue. I have not found another program that can offer the same quality content related ads. The down side is that Google ad revenue is historically not

| April 2005 | Apr 21 | Payment issued - details | | ($2,007.94) | |
|---|---|---|---|---|---|
| | Apr 30 | Earnings (Apr 1 - Apr 30) - details | $2,329.08 | | |
| | **Balance at end of April** ? | | | | $2,329.08 |
| May 2005 | May 24 | Payment issued - details | | ($2,329.08) | |
| | May 31 | Earnings (May 1 - May 31) - details | $3,560.58 | | |
| | **Balance at end of May** ? | | | | $3,560.58 |
| June 2005 | Jun 23 | Payment issued - details | | ($3,560.58) | |
| | Jun 30 | Earnings (Jun 1 - Jun 30) - details | $4,896.98 | | |
| | **Balance at end of June** ? | | | | $4,896.98 |
| July 2005 | Jul 22 | Payment issued - details | | ($4,896.98) | |
| | Jul 31 | Earnings (Jul 1 - Jul 31) - details | $3,230.57 | | |
| | **Balance at end of July** ? | **$4,896.98** | | | $3,230.57 |

**$3,230.57**

*Image above: Google pay per click ad revenue for a two month period. Note the monthly earnings are over $3000.00 per month. This profit is from Pay Per Click ads and does not include any other profit center revenue.*

---

dependable. Google can, and often does, seemingly overnight change your payout rates and drastically effect your websites daily earnings. I still highly recommend Google but warn all web masters not to rely solely on Google Adsense for your profit. Diversify by using other PPC programs, set up affiliate programs, and develop your own products or services. This way if your Google pay per click profits drop 50% overnight your online business will not be completely devastated.

Please note: Never put other contextual ads on the same page with Google ads. This would violate Google's regulations and may result in you being dropped from the program. You should also restrict the number of ads per page. One to two ads is the general rule.

---

Below are a list of other Pay Per Click vendors. This is not a complete list but rather just a small sample of some of the more popular programs. I highly advise an 80/ 20 mix. Put Google ads on 80% of your pages and other PPC ads on the balance.

AdBright                    http://www.adbrite.com/mb/
AdBrite can help you monetize your site with advertising that fits the content and user base of your web page. Once your site is approved, you just insert a code onto your page. AdBrights base of advertisers includes top brands like Live Nation, GM, AT&T and Verizon—at the same time, AdBrite serves ads on nearly 1 billion pages daily, providing massive scale opportunities. In addition, you can choose to approve or reject ads before they appear on your site. They pay you monthly once you reach the $100 minimum.

BidVertiser                 http://www.adbrite.com/mb/
Join BidVertiser now and they will help to turn the advertising space on your web page into cash! Simply display the BidVertiser text ads on your website and let advertisers bid against each other! They will always display the highest bidders to maximize your revenue so you will make more money. With this program you get paid for every visitor that clicks on an ad. BidVestisers goal is to enable you to make as much as possible from your advertising space, They pay monthly, either by check, or instantly through PayPal

RevenuePilot                http://www.revenuepilot.com/
RevenuePilot provides you with innovative, efficient and effective ways to monetize your traffic. Pay For Performance (PFP) and the Pay Per Click (PPC) markets have created ample opportunity for the web

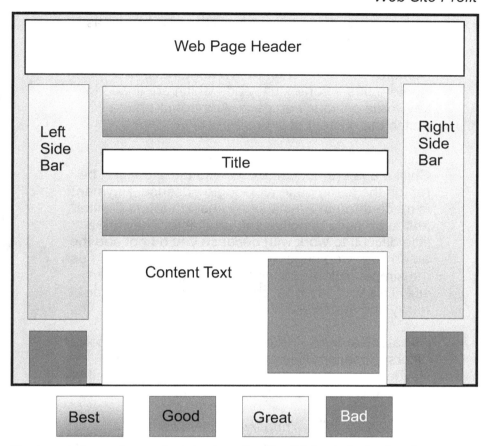

*The layout above shows where to place Pay Per Click ads for best performance.*

masters to turn its traffic into profits. RevenuePilot offers its affiliates seamless entrance into this highly profitable arena through its Premiere Pay Per Click Network

Text-Link-Ads          http://www.text-link-ads.com/
Once approved, you can run simple text ads on your site. Payments are made via Paypal or Clickbank. You earn a  50% commission of the sale price for each ad. Text-link-ads is not considered contextual advertising

so its is acceptable to be run on the same page as Google Adsense ads.

Kontera                    http://www.kontera.com/
Kontera offers contextually ads which are linked to keywords on your web page. Ads from Kontera will match the content of your site.

Chitika.com                http://chitika.com/
Chitika ads are not contextual and therefore can be run on the same page as Google Adsense. Payment is made through Paypal or by check. I found Chitika ads to be quite effective and profitable. They are a little difficult to work with because you do not see the ad on your web page after inserting HTML code. I use the simple trick of placing html inside a table on my site. This way when Im changing page layout I can easily find the chitika html code.

AffiliatesGarage      http://www.affiliatesgarage.com/
Offers  Adsense Style ads  with  Clickbank and Paydotcom text ads that you can place on your site or blog and earn up to 75% commission.

Miva                       http://www.miva.com/
Miva offers a wide variety of ad formats that your can utilize on your web site. They have content ads, inline ads, and search ads. Webmasters are paid on a per click basis. Payments are made monthly by check or through  Paypal.

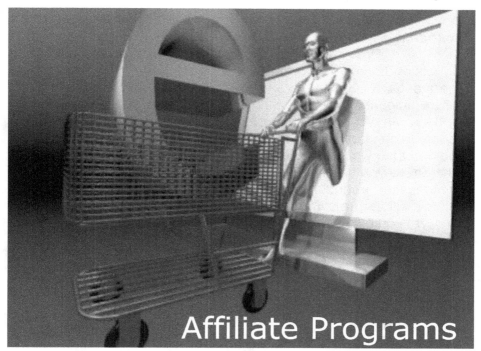

Affiliate Programs

*Affiliate programs are an excellent way to enhance or supplement a web sites earning potential. Image courtesy AllPosters.com. See Affiliate section for additional information on how you can profit from these photographs and art images.*

## Affiliate Programs

Affiliate programs are an excellent way to enhance or supplement a web site's earning potential. Listed below are a variety of Affiliate programs. You should search these sites for associated products to market on your site. Most are set up so that you earn a commission for each item sold. I also included links to a few of my own pages which have affiliate adds. You are invited to click around and see for yourself how a few well placed affiliate ads can enhance your site while providing another separate profit center.

### *Clickbank*

Promote and sell your own products or promote other products and receive a commission on each sale which you generate. Click Bank is a great affiliate program. You can create your own digital product or sell products created by others. Either way it's a win win situation. For example, if you author your own ebook you can post it on click bank. Affiliates will then market your ebook on their web sites for a commission that you set. If your not that creative you can choose from a huge assortment of downloadable products and build ads for them on your own web site. You will earn a commission, usually 50-75% of each item sold. Better yet you can do both.

Check out the link listed below. This is the click bank landing page for two Home Security ebooks I authored. Basically, anyone with a website can sign up as a click bank affiliate and sell either or both of these books. My affiliates earn 70% profit for each book sold.

http://www.homesafetyt oday.net/homesecurityb ook.htm?hop=0

The add to cart button at bottom of ad brings customers directly to clickbanks payment page. Clickbank sends all affiliates a check every two weeks.

**The Ultimate Guide to**
## Home Security
PDF eBook
*By Daniel Berg*

This 58 page 6"x9" full color e-book is packed with information, hardware and systems designed for homeowners to help you protect your home form a burglary. Mr Berg has covered all the basics and includes proven tips so you can easily transform your home from a burglary target to a safe sanctuary for your family and property. This text is packed with detailed information on which locks are best, how to obtain the best window or door security. Book includes sections on sky Lights, garage & sheds security, attached garages, alarm systems, panic buttons, wireless alarm systems and much more. Do not go out and purchase any expensive hardware or alarm system before first reading this how to guide. This text should be mandatory reading for any homeowner looking to keep family and property safe. *Image right: sample page*

**Add To Cart**

only $9.95 instant download, printable PDF file

*Image Right: An add from one of the authors web pages. The ad promotes a downloadable e-book which is one of Clickbank's affiliate products. The "Add to Cart" button brings customers directly to Clickbank's payment page.*

Check out all of the author's scuba related downloadable clickbank products.
http://www.aquaexplorers.com/e_books_downloadable.htm

Above is an add from one of my web pages. The ad promotes a downloadable e-book which is one of Clickbank's affiliate products. The "Add to Cart" button brings customers directly to Clickbank's payment page. Anyone with a website that has visitors interested in Home Security can become a Clickbank affiliate, copy images and product information and promote this book on their own website. Click bank affiliates usually earn 50%- 70% per sale.

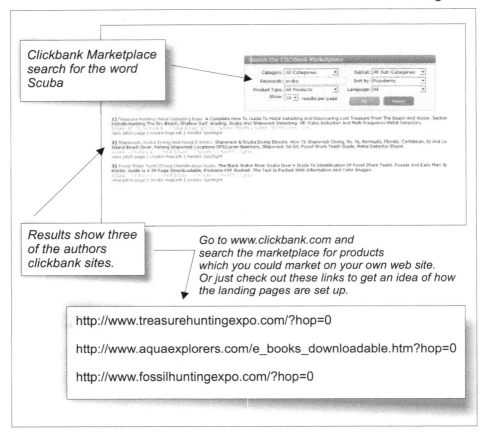

Image above: Is of the Clickbank Marketplace after a search for "scuba". Prospective affiliates can search for any topic while looking for appropriate downloadable products to market on their own web sites. Once you find a Clickbank product you want to market just 1) Join Clickbank (it's free). 2) Copy and paste product image onto your website 3) Create a link to the image which contains your Clickbank ID. 4) Sit back and collect your profits. You can earn up to 70% profit. Clickbank will send you a check every two weeks.

### AllPosters.com

AllPosters is another excellent affiliate program which can be used by almost all webmasters. You can sell posters and art work on your website, and earn 25% commission on each poster sold. Not only can you add a variety of product links, banners and search button links, but as an affiliate you can also use images from AllPosters to enhance your web site. AllPosters has a huge assortment of art available so it's easy to find affiliated art work to promote. Affiliate products can be linked to directly or affiliates can add search buttons so their viewers can search for any subject. I have used many of their posters as images on my web pages and also sell the same art posters to my customers.

Check out any search topic and see if AllPosters has an appropriate poster for you to market on your own web site.

Check out any search topic and see if AllPosters has appropriate poster for you to market on your own web site.

Sample link the author set up on one of his web pages to promote AllPosters affiliate sales. Image courtesy AllPosters.com.

## *Commision Junction*
Here is yet another affiliate program that offers a huge variety of products. Most web masters should be able to find associated products that will compliment your existing product line nicely while providing another profit center for your internet business.

### *From www.cj.com:*
*Maximize your revenue opportunities by developing sustainable relationships with top-tier advertisers. Perform and get paid for every sale and lead you generate. For qualifying publishers, take your program to the next level with our industry exclusive solution for top-performers. Apply to join advertisers' programs, get immediate access to their entire inventory of links and begin placing their offers on your websites, in e-mail campaigns, or in search listings. In addition, strategic advice and featured weekly advertiser offers are available through CJU Online, our comprehensive online resource. Click here to join our unparalleled network of publishers and learn more about our commitment to the long-term success of top-performing publishers.*

Note the pay per click Google ads

Suggested reading page with books from Amazon's affiliate program.

## Amazon.com

Amazon has an unique affiliate program called Amazon Associates. Web masters can earn up to 15% commission on a wide variety of products. Just visit Amazon.com and click on the Join Associates link at the bottom of the main page. Although Amazon Associates are best known for its affiliate book program I would strongly suggest spending some time on this site and finding a few non book products. What I have done on several of my sites is to create a "suggested reading" page. That page has a google PPC ad and an assortment of topic related affiliate books from Amazon. The

Sample of other products available from Amazon's Affiliate program.

page is simple to produce and consistently produces profit. In addition, I have been able to capitalize on some other higher retail price products that Amazon offers like cameras. Here are a few hints for Amazon Associates:

1) When setting up your amazon associate program make sure you select direct deposit so you avoid the payment processing fee.

2) Your website should be up and running before you register, as Amazon will review the site manually before approval.

3) When it's time to start building links add the Link Builder header to the top of Amazon's page. This will make it extremely easy to search for products and build links with your affiliate ID already built in. See Amazon's instructions for more information.

4) Try out Amazon's A-store. You can find a link to it when signed into your associate account. Basically, the A-store is a simple way to set up an affiliate product page. The store provides templates and is very easy and fast to set up. I have used the A-store to create Suggested Reading pages. Check out links below for samples.

Bottle Collecting:
http://astore.amazon.com/shipwrecks-20?_encoding=UTF8&node=19

Metal Detecting:
http://astore.amazon.com/treasurehuntingexpo-20

**e-Book Marketing and Publishing**

*Courtesy Allposters.com*

### e-Book Marketing and Publishing

Webmasters basically have three ways to profit from eBooks. What makes these items so enticing is that once set up you never have to think about them again. No boxes to pack or product to ship. Just sit back and deposit your check every two weeks.

### Marketing existing eBooks

The first way to profit from ebooks would be to market an existing eBook that corresponds to your websites content. Marketing eBooks is a great way to increase the profit of any web page. There are several online companies that offer eBooks as affiliate products. I highly recommend Clickbank. They have a huge assortment of eBooks and offer commissions up to 75% for each book sold. Basically, it should be a no brainier. Up to 75% profit with no inventory cost and no shipping and handling hassles. Most brick and mortar retailers do not make anywhere near that type of mark-up. Whether you have an existing web site or are now publishing a new site I highly recommend placing a few links to affiliate ebook products. You may have to try a few to find which products sell well

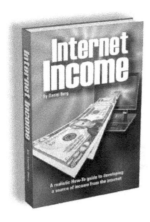

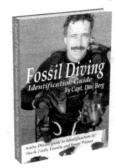

*Check out an assortment of the authors PDF fomat downloadable ebooks. All of these books are available through Clickbank.*

http://www.treasurehuntingexpo.com
http://www.fossilhuntingexpo.com
http://www.homesafetytoday.net/homesecuritybook.htm
http://www.aquaexplorers.com/e_books_downloadable.htm

on your site but once that is done you can then just sit back and count your money.

## Publish you own eBook

If you are an expert in any field or have access to information that others would find worthwhile then you should consider authoring a downloadable PDF format e-book. Many webmasters have already produced the majority of text for an eBook product while writing the unique content for web pages. Creating a unique e-book will give you a product which you can sell on your web page, market through online auctions and market through your own affiliate network. Remember, other than the time and effort used during creation, eBooks do not cost you anything to produce. Unlike conventional printing where you have up-front printing and inventory cost, with eBooks every sale is 100% profit. Once finished, you can also take the same PDF file and have it printed into a soft or hardcover book -

*(see Print on demand book publishing).* In addition, you can offer the same text in a downloadable Kindle electronic reader format. Now you have three unique products which you can sell or which can be offered to affiliates to market. Marketing an ebook through affiliates is easy. All you have to do is sign up to a program like Clickbank. Anyone with a web site can then search Cickbanks Marketplace for affiliate products of interest to their clients. Affiliates (other web masters) will then market your eBook on their own web sites. This will drastically increasing your product's exposure. They make a commission on each unit sold and you make profit not only from the products sold but also from the increased traffic to your web site.

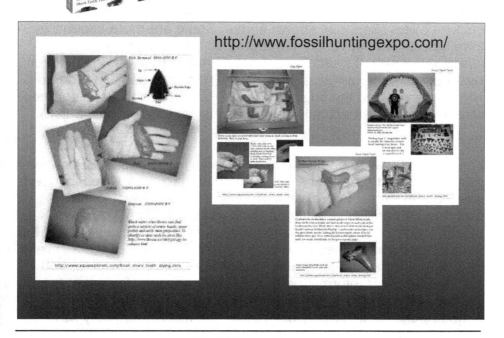

*Note that the interior of the authors ebooks are laid out like a quality full color perfect bound book. Unlike many eBooks on the market that only have text, these products are packed with color photos and images. Bottom line is your customers will never be disappointed with quality products.*

http://www.fossilhuntingexpo.com/

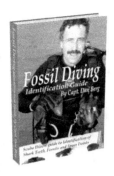
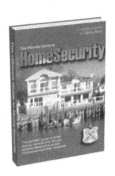

Check out some of my books which were published as ebooks and marketed on my own websites as well as through clickbanks affiliate program. There are many programs and online sources to create 3d eBook covers like those shown above. Some are more expensive than others. I highly recommend graphic artist Aaron Hirsh (www.aerox.net). It's simple, just e-mail Aaron your photo and title text, he will respond with a price quote. After payment is made he will then email you the finished art. Unlike traditional online sources, with Aerox you can actually communicate with the graphic artist.

I use Corel Draw to do all the page layouts in my books. But many graphic or word processing programs have the capabilities to insert images and export PDF files. I use Corel because that is the program I'm familiar with. If you think you want to put your own eBook together I would recommend that you look through any of the above listed texts to see how each page is designed. Take a careful look at the photo sub titles, image placement, and text fonts. You can then use this information or duplicate the style. Note that the interior of these books are laid out like quality full color perfect bound books. Unlike many eBooks on the market that only have

text, these products are packed with color photos and images. The bottom line is that customers should never be disappointed. Also note that on PDF ebooks you can insert links to promote your own website, products or services. Basically, for each book sold your are also gaining a visitor to your web page.

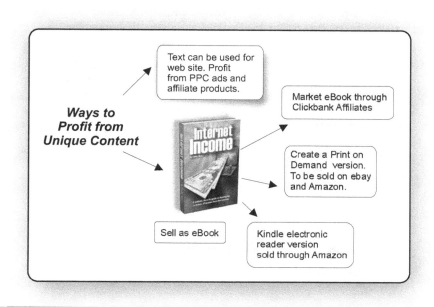

**The Best of Both Worlds**

Why limit yourself? Why not become a Clickbank affiliate and market existing eBooks as well as producing and marketing your own title?

Lets recap and take a look at possible eBook profit.

> *Your eBook sold on your own web site -100% profit*
> *Affiliate eBook sold on your web site -50-75% commission*
> *Your eBook sold on Ebay and delivered on CD-80% profit*
> *Your eBook sold by a Clickbank affiliate- 25-50% profit*
> *Your print on demand book sold on your web site -70-80% profit*
> *Your printed on demand book marketed by LuLu -shared profit*
> *Create a Kindle electronic reader version -sold through Amazon*
> *That is at least 6 ways to create consistent profit from just one product!*

It does not take long for a few sales to add up to significant monthly earnings. For example sell just four eBooks per day @ 9.95/ea =$1000.00/Month

At $9.95/book retail you only have to sell 3-4 books per day to create $1000/month profit. Remember you will have no printing, shipping or inventory expenses. Add to that the fact the affiliates will be marketing your book through their own web sites. You do the work once then get to sit back and collect the rewards.

**Clickbank** Promote and sell your own products or promote other products and receive a commission on each sale which you generate. Click Bank is a great affiliate program. You can create your own digital product or sell products created by others. Either way its a win win situation. For example, if you author your own eBook you can post it on ClickBank. Affiliates will then market your eBook on their web sites for a commission that you set. If your not that creative you can choose from a huge assortment of downloadable products and build ads for them on your own web site. You will earn a commission, usually 50-75% of each item sold.

---

Check out the link listed below. This is the ClickBank landing page for two Home Security eBooks I authored. Basically, anyone with a web site can sign up as a ClickBank affiliate and sell either or both of these books. My affiliates earn 70% profit for each book sold. Note the Google Adsence ad on the same page.

http://www.homesafetytoday.net/homesecuritybook.htm?hop=0

The add to cart button at bottom of the ad brings customers directly to Clickbank's payment page. Clickbank sends all affiliates a check every two weeks.

**Kindle** *(Amazons electronic book reader)*

Kindle is Amazon.com's version of an electronic paper, or electronic book reader device. The device's display is designed to mimic the appearance of ordinary ink on paper. Unlike a conventional flat panel display, which uses a back light to illuminate its screen the Kindle display reflects light like paper. Amazon has now provided ebook authors with another way to earn profits. Amazon has set up Kindle publishing. Basically, eBook authors can convert their eBooks into a Kindle version. For all text books this is a fairly simple process, but for books that are heavily illustrated it is a bit more difficult. At the time of this writing its still a little difficult to automatically convert PDF files. Basically, the kindle device allows users to change font size. This means that the books pages can not be designed like a printed book with text wrapped around photos. There are several online services available that will convert PDF files into HTML code. Unfortunately, these services can be a bit expensive. The quote I received for converting one of my PDF eBooks to Kindle was over $300. Instead of paying for the conversion I opted to create my own Kindle version. The process was pretty easy. I used Microsoft Word which is one of the programs which Kindle can convert to its' Digital Text Format. I copied and pasted all of the text for my book directly into Microsoft Word. I then opened the PDF version of the book and used Adobe's snapshot feature to copy and paste each photo into its' relative position. Do not worry about photo quality. The Kindle device only displays in black and white and photo resolution is not the best. After that I created a glossary and used bookmarks that allow the end user to jump to any section of the text. Final step was to go into Kindle Publishing and upload the file which also converts it to a Digital Text Format. Once reviewed and accepted Amazon will market the product and authors will earn a commissions on every Kindle book sold. I sold a book the very first day it was listed on Amazon's Kindle store.

*The authors Wreck Valley book as a Kindle electronic reader product.*

*LuLu sales, page for one of the authors print on demand books. This book can be marketed through your own web site, through LuLu or through online auctions. In all cases you do not have to inventory any items. Once an order is received just place an order with LuLu and have the item sent directly to your customer.*

## Print on demand Publishing

Books are a great product for web sites as well as online auctions. If designed correctly, they can also promote your website. Now anyone with a little expertise and the desire to write, can self-publish a book without incurring a huge printing expense and without having to inventory any product. The service is called print on demand printing. I have used LuLu as a print on demand printer and have been very happy with their service.

Image above: LuLu search page result showing one of the author's print on demand titles. These books can be marketed on your own website through online sellers like amazon or on online auctions.

Lulu.com                    http://www.lulu.com/
Free print on demand service which enables you to publish, print and sell books, calendars, music, etc. on demand. There are no setup fees. Each book is ordered and printed individually. I have used LuLu to create a hard copy of an existing ebook. The process was pretty easy and I was very happy with the printed book. I opted for a full color cover with black and white interior. LuLu gives you the option of creating add to cart buttons. By adding a description and photo to my web site I quickly started to sell my LuLu created

softcover book. The best part is that unlike conventional printers, I did not have to purchase or stock a few thousand books.

Check out the ad listed above. This "Secret Bookcase Door Plans" book was originally created as an ebook and sells quite well on ClickBank (see affiliate Sales). My website customers now have the choice of buying this title as a downloadable ebook or in a perfect bound soft cover version through LuLu. Either way, I make a commission on every book sold and do not have to ship orders or inventory product.

*Print on demand books can be perfect bound, spiral or staple bound. Print on demand books can have black and white or full color interiors. One of the best features with LuLu as a print on demand publisher is that your book can also be available for sale on Amazon.com and other online retailers.*

http://www.treasurehuntingexpo.com/

## CafePress

At CafePress.com, you can create and sell a variety of customizable print on demand products with zero up front costs and zero inventory investment. You can sell merchandise you design including t-shirts, posters, mugs, bumper stickers and much more. CafePress will give you a FREE online shop to promote your products. CafePress handles all payment transactions including major credit cards. They will ship your products worldwide and manages all returns/exchanges. They even offer customer service via toll-free phone and email. Best of all they send you a monthly check for your earnings.          http://www.cafepress.com/

*Check out a variety of the authors CafePress products.*
*http://www.cafepress.com/wreckvalleyshop*

*Online auctions are a great way to make some extra money and promote your web site. Image courtesy AllPosters.com. See affiliate section for additional information on how you can profit from these photographs and art images.*

## Online Auctions

Online auctions are a great way to make some extra money and promote your website. eBay is a perfect example. Sellers can list an assortment of items with images. If you have a product you can continually repeat the ad. Not only will you profit from direct sales but if you place links to your web site with your ad you will increase traffic to your site.

Instead of typing the product info into ebays auction page. I design my eBay ads on my web design program ( I use Microsoft's Front Page). Any design program will work. The benefit is that you can copy and paste the HTML code directly into eBay. Not only will this save a bit of time but your ad can include images, background design and video without having to upload images to eBay. Basically ads will look better and are just easier to manage.

*A variety of the authors print on demand books available through LuLu. Note that all of these titles were originally released as PDF format ebooks are available to be sold by Clickbank Affiliates as ebooks. As soft cover books these titles can be marketed on ebay and other online auctions.*

Above is a list of some of the author's print on demand books available through LuLu. Note that all of these titles were originally released as PDF format eBooks. Since these books are now available as perfect bound soft cover titles they can now be marketed through Amazon.com, online auctions like eBay and through other online retailers.

*Online auctions are a great way to make some extra money and promote your web site. Ebay is a perfect example. Sellers can list an assortment of items with images.*

In the past we could market ebooks on eBay, with excellent results. EBay's new policy prohibits downloadable products from the auction. Ebooks can still be marketed on ebay, but now you will have to download them onto a CD and ship the CD to the auction winner. Another idea would be to have your ebook printed into a soft cover book. There are print on demand companies where this can be done at no cost. You can market the printed version of the book on eBay. Whenever an ebay auction ends with a sale you just order the book and have it sent directly from the printer to your ebay customer.

*Note: 100% Positive feedback. Positive feedback is very important for ebay sellers.*

*Two of the authors print on demand books. Which are sold through the authors web sites as well as on Ebay.*

Ebay has recently banned downloadable products from its auctions. Sellers can still use the service to market eBooks but now have to offer them as a file saved to a CD and shipped to buyer or as a print on demand title, shipped as a perfect bound book.

*Print on demand books can be printed with full color or with black and white interior images. The publisher also offers a variety of binding options.*

*Courtesy Allposters.com*

## Web Commerce

### e-Commerce

Website tools webmasters can use to add online shopping cart features to your website. These tools make it easy to sell your products on the internet.

osCommerce

Everything you need to get started in selling physical and digital goods over the internet, from the catalog that is presented to your customers, to the administration tools that completely handles your products, customers, orders, and online store data. osCommerce Online Merchant is an Open Source online shop e-commerce solution that is available for free under the GNU General Public License. It features a rich set of out-of-the-box online shopping cart functionality that allows store owners to set up, run, and maintain online stores with minimum effort and with no costs, fees, or limitations involved.

*www.WebMoneyExpo.com*

*Courtesy Allposters.com*

## Virtual Cash

Websites and online auctions are often enhanced by accepting multiple payment options. Virtual Cash systems are an excellent and immediate method to pay or accept payments. I have used PayPal as a form of auction payment for years. In addition, PayPal offers some ecommerce tools like "pay now" and "add to cart" buttons that allow webmasters to accept PayPal or credit card payments for any website marketed product.

PayPal                    www.paypal.com

PayPal is the faster, safer way to pay and get paid online. The service allows members to send money without sharing financial information, with the flexibility to pay using their account balances, bank accounts, credit cards or personal financing. With more than 75 million active accounts in 190 markets and 19 currencies around the world, PayPal enables global ecommerce. PayPal is an eBay company and is made up of three leading online payment services: the PayPal global payments platform, the Payflow Gateway, and Bill Me Later. Paypal is an online payment system which uses virtual cash. Transactions are instantaneous. PayPal also accepts credit card payments.


E-gold          http://www.egold.com/
E-gold is an electronic currency and online payment system based on real gold. E-gold is integrated into an account based payment system that empowers people to use gold as money. Specifically, the e-gold payment system enables people to spend specified weights of gold to other e-gold accounts. Only the ownership changes - the gold in the treasury grade vault stays.

*Free Clipart image*

## Free clipart and Images

Below you will find a list of websites that offer free clipart. These images can be used to enhance your website, products or ads.

AllFreeClipart.com
Here at All Free ClipArt you'll find a fast growing collection of thousands of high quality clipart for free. You're free to use the clipart in this collection for personal pages and whatever else you'd like, the graphics are royalty free clipart. Thousands of royalty-free clipart images.

BabysBacks.com
Over 10,000 images, backgrounds, bullets, headers, bars, webmaster essential logos, buttons, clip-art, animations, and more!

Barry's Clipart
Many categories of free clipart for download.

Clip Art Of.com
Free comic clipart.

Clip-art.com
Comprehensive directory of clip-art and images.

Download-Free-Clipart
A collection of links to free clipart download sites.

*Free Clipart image*

Free Clip Art.com
You can download high quality Vector and Web-Ready clipart for FREE. Ready-made pieces of printable art, such as illustrations, borders, and cartoons, that can be electronically copied and used to decorate your documents or projects.

Free-Clipart-Pictures.net
Dozens of free clip art categories that have fairly large images. There are also galleries of myspace stuff such as, layouts, backgrounds and glitter graphics. If you are looking for larger collections on the net, then you can visit high quality sites just below to find related resources such as free clipart, animated graphics, photos, fonts and desktop themes.

FreeClipartNow.com
A large collection of high quality, public domain clipart graphics for presentations, web pages, documents, emails.

Gif.com
Search collection of more than 17,000 quality free clipart images. No pop ups, no tricks.

Gifworld
A world of FREE GIFs, animated GIFs, fonts, photo's, etc.

Graphxkingdom
Graphxkingdom, home to thousands of free clipart, icons, backgrounds, bars, interfaces, and other cool, free graphics.

JAC Clipart Archive

Large collection of public domain images, clipart organized by category.

Open Clipart
This project aims to create an archive of user contributed clip art that can be freely used.

Public Domain Clip Art
A HUGE collection of public domain clip art. The collection is FREE and NO REGISTRATION is required.

Totally free clipart
There's a lot in here (well over 3000 handpicked images at last count), so sit back, relax and take your time. Feel free to either browse the graphics by selecting one of the main categories below, or using the menu. If you know exactly what kind of image you're looking for, there's a search. 100% free clipart, no pop ups, trick links or registration required.

Webshots
Large directory of high-quality images and wallpapers for use on your desktop. The images are free, but you need to signup first (also free).

WiseGorilla
Free educational clip art and links to other quality free educational clip art sites.

*Courtesy Allposters.com*

## Get Paid to take online surveys

You do not need a website or product to sell in order to make money on the internet. Below is a list of companies that pay you to take online surveys. This is not a complete list of online survey companies but rather just a sample.

American Consumer Opinion
Get paid for sharing your opinions and ideas in online surveys. Win money in monthly drawings just for being a member. Win money in drawings when you fill out a a short questionnaire. Earn cash each time you complete a survey (a longer questionnaire).

GlobalTestMarket.com
Earn cash by filling out surveys and referring friends.

goZing surveys
In return for participating in online and/or telephone surveys, you receive Amazon.com gift certificates or PayPal cash.

I-SpeakUp.com
$50 for filling out 25-minute surveys, $150 for participating in focus group panels for 30 to 60 minutes, earn free trips, free dinners, get freebies given to you with each survey completed.

Online-Paid-Surveys.net
A free site where users can share experiences and learn about online paid survey opportunities. The site includes a user blog, polls, a user review section, and editorial reviews on legitimate paid market research opportunities.

Opinion Outpost
Opinion Outpost is an online community where people like you can come to share their opinions by participating in survey research. In return for your valued opinion, you can earn opinion points which can be exchanged for cash and prizes.

Pureprofile
Get paid for responding to messages and participating in surveys.

SurveySavvy.com
Earn cash by filling out surveys and referring friends.

YellowSurveys.com
Over 500 survey companies offering paid surveys in cash and prizes.

Below is a list of
companies that pay you
to read emails and surf
the web.Image courtesy
AllPosters.com. See
Affiliate section for
additional information on
how you can profit from
these photographs and
art images.

## Get Paid to Surf the Web and Read Email

You do not need to produce or maintain a website or have product to sell in order to make money on the internet. Below is a list of companies that pay you to read emails and surf the web. Please note that is is not a complete list but rather a sample of potential profitable services individuals can provide to earn money at home. No claims are made about the below listed sites. The information is only a sample of web surfing opportunities.

BountyCenter
Get paid to read emails, click on banners and refer friends.

Hits 4 Pay
Get paid to read emails, click on banners and refer friends.

E-Mail Paus U
Get paid to read email and for visiting Websites.

Wow Earnings
Get paid to read emails, click on banners and refer friends.

# Glossary of Terms

### Blog -- (weB LOG)
*A blog is basically a journal that is available on the web. The activity of updating a blog is "blogging" and someone who keeps a blog is a "blogger."*

### Download
*Transferring data (usually a file) from another computer to the computer you are are using. The opposite of upload.*

### HTML -- (HyperText Markup Language)
*The coding language used to create Hypertext documents for use on the World Wide Web.*

### KEYWORD(S)
*A word searched for in a search command. Keywords are searched in any order. Use spaces to separate keywords in simple keyword searching.*

### Meta Tag
*A specific kind of HTML tag that contains information not normally displayed to the user. Meta tags contain information about the page itself, hence the name ("meta" means "about this subject").*

### PDF or .pdf or pdf file
*Abbreviation for Portable Document Format, a file format developed by Adobe Systems, that is used to capture almost any kind of document with the formatting in the original. Viewing a PDF file requires Acrobat Reader*

### PPC  (Pay Per Click)
Pay or get paid for every click to an advertisement.

### SEO -- (Search Engine Optimization)
*The practice of designing web pages so that they rank as high as possible in search results from search engines.*

### TITLE (of a document)
*The official title of a document from the "meta" field called title. The text of this meta title field may or may not also occur in the visible body of the document. It is what appears in the top bar of the window when you display the document and it is the title that appears in search engine results.*

---

Web page
*A document designed for viewing in a web browser. Typically written in HTML. A web site is made of one or more web pages.*

Website
*The entire collection of web pages and other information (such as images, sound, and video files, etc.) that are made available through what appears to users as a single web server. Typically, all the of pages in a website share the same basic URL.*

The author invites your to check out a few of his websites and see examples of how the principles detailed in this text are used.

http://www.treasurehuntingexpo.com/
http://www.fossilhuntingexpo.com/ — *Clickbank Landing Pages*

http://www.aquaexplorers.com/e_books_downloadable.htm — *ebooks*

http://www.homesafetytoday.net/
http://www.webmoneyexpo.com/ — *PPC ads*

http://www.thewaterfrontexpo.com/nauticalart.htm — *All Posters affiliate program*

http://www.shipwreckexpo.com/books_shipwreck_suggested.htm

*Amazon suggested reading page*

*The above listed links are just a small sample of what you can do. Set up the basics and start creating Internet Income. Then experiment with other affiliate programs, products and advertising programs.*